Wild Predators!

Deadly Insects

Heinemann
LIBRARY

Andrew Solway

www.heinemann.co.uk/library
Visit our website to find out more information about **Heinemann Library** books.

To order:
 Phone 44 (0) 1865 888066
Send a fax to 44 (0) 1865 314091
 Visit the Heinemann Bookshop at www.heinemann.co.uk/library to browse our catalogue and order online.

First published in Great Britain by
Heinemann Library, Halley Court, Jordan Hill,
Oxford OX2 8EJ, part of Harcourt Education.
Heinemann is a registered trademark of Harcourt
Education Ltd.

Editorial: Nancy Dickmann, Tanvi Rai and Sarah
Chappelow
Design: David Poole and Calcium
Illustrations: Geoff Ward
Picture Research: Maria Joannou and Catherine
Bevan
Production: Camilla Smith

Originated by Ambassador Litho Ltd.
Printed and bound in China by
South China Printing Company.
The paper used to print this book comes from
sustainable resources.

ISBN 0 431 19003 8
08 07 06 05
10 9 8 7 6 5 4 3 2 1

British Library Cataloguing in Publication Data
Solway, Andrew
Deadly Insects. – (Wild predators)
  599.7'73153
A full catalogue record for this book is available
from the British Library.

Acknowledgements
The Publishers would like to thank the following
for permission to reproduce photographs:
ANT Photo Library p. **40 bottom** (Fredy Mercay);
Ardea pp. **8** (Steve Hopkin), **13** (Eric Lindgren),
21 bottom (Pascal Goetgheluck), **23** (Ken Hoy),
26 (Steve Hopkin), **28** (Pascal Goetgheluck), **31**
(John Cancalosi), **34** (Alan Weaving), **35** (Alan
Weaving), **38** (Ian Beames); Corbis pp. **5 top**
(Neil Miller/Papilio), **5 bottom** (James L Amos),
14 (Anthony Bannister/Gallo Images), **39**
(George D Lepp), **42** (Chris Hellier), **43** (Anthony
Bannister); FLPA pp. **6** (B Borrell Casais), **7**
bottom, **9** (Ian Rose), **12** (Larry West), **21 top**
(Treat Davidson), **25** (Tony Wharton), **30** (Hans
Dieter Brand), **32** (Larry West), **33 top** (Larry
West), **36 top** (Jeremy Early), **36 bottom**
(Winifried Wisniewski), **37** (Fritz Polking), **41** (B
Borrell Casais); Holt Studios p. **33 bottom**;
NHPA pp. **7 top** (Stephen Dalton), **11** (Stephen
Dalton), **16** (Stephen Dalton), **18** (Simon Colmer),
24 (Stephen Dalton), **29** (James Carmichael Jr);
Oxford Scientific Films pp. **10** (Roland Mayr), **15**
top (James H Robson), **17** (Alistair MacEwen),
19 (David M Dennis), **20** (James H Robinson), **22**
(Brian Kenney); Premaphotos Wildlife p. **4**;
Science Photo Library p. **40 top** (Dr Morley
Read).

Cover photograph of a praying mantis
eating prey reproduced with permission of
NHPA/Stephen Dalton.

The Publishers would like to thank Michael Bright
of the BBC Natural History Unit for his
assistance in the preparation of this book.

Contents

Any words appearing in the text in bold, **like this**, are explained in the Glossary.

Six-legged killers

When we think about **predators**, we often think of animals such as tigers and sharks rather than insects. However, if we were a couple of centimetres tall or smaller, we might think differently! Wherever we lived, from deep in the soil to high in the treetops, there would be insect predators about, with weapons such as biting or stabbing jaws, a sting full of deadly poison, or spiny legs for grabbing.

Insects are the most successful animals on the planet. There are more known **species** (kinds) of insect than of all the other animals together.

Cuticle

One key to the insects' success is their **cuticle**. Insects use it in an amazing variety of ways. Like our bones, cuticle is strong, and is used to support the insect's body. Cuticle is also light and waterproof. Thick cuticle is tough, and is used for jaws, claws, and for protective armour. Thin cuticle is flexible, and is used in joints and to line the gut.

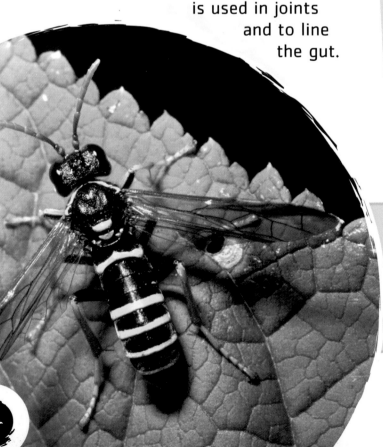

Insect relatives

Insects belong to a group of animals called arthropods, along with spiders, crustaceans (crabs, shrimps, and related animals), and myriapods (centipedes and millipedes). All arthropods have a tough outer skeleton to keep their body in shape.

Insects are arthropods with six legs, one pair of antennae, and a body divided into three parts – the head, the thorax, and the abdomen. Many insects also have wings.

The larvae of saw flies are very different from the adult insects. When an insect changes from a larva to a pupa to an adult, it is called complete metamorphosis.

Wings

Another key to the success of insects is their wings. Some insects (for instance ones that live underground) do not have wings but the majority of insects have wings as adults. With wings, insects are able to travel further and faster. Predators with wings can hunt food in the air, and escape predators themselves.

Life changes

In some insects, such as grasshoppers, the young insects (called **nymphs**) look similar to adults but have no wings. The nymphs change gradually into adults over a number of **moults**. This is called **gradual metamorphosis**.

Other insects begin life as a **larva** – for instance a grub or a caterpillar. The larva feeds and grows, then produces a hard case or spins a **cocoon** to become a **pupa**. Inside its protective case or cocoon, the pupa changes. When the pupa splits open, an adult insect emerges. This is called **complete metamorphosis**.

One problem with the cuticle is that it does not grow. Insects get round this problem by moulting (shedding their old cuticle) as they get bigger, like this **cicada**.

Dragonflies

It is a summer evening by a slow backwater in southern England. As the sun sets, clouds of **midges** gather like smoke over the water. Darting through the midge clouds comes a much larger flier, flicking from side to side as it snaps up its midge **prey**. A stray sunbeam across the water catches the dragonfly in flight, lighting it up like a brilliant jewel.

The dragonfly family is made up of two groups, the dragonflies and the damselflies. True dragonflies are large, brightly coloured, fast-flying insects with two pairs of wings. The front wings are slightly smaller than the hind ones, and while resting the dragonfly holds them out horizontally. Damselflies are slimmer than dragonflies. Their front and rear wings are the same, and they hold their wings vertically when resting. True dragonflies and damselflies are both fierce **predators**.

Underwater larvae

Dragonflies lay their eggs in water, and the **larvae** are underwater predators. Dragonfly larvae have structures like a fish's gills that allow them to breathe underwater. The larvae are not fussy eaters – they will eat any animal they can catch. Their prey includes tadpoles, small fish, and even other dragonfly larvae. Some larvae stalk their prey, while others wait for prey to come to them.

Unlike other insects, which either beat both pairs of wings together or use only one pair for flying, dragonflies can beat their front and back wings independently.

Different dragonfly larvae live in all kinds of watery habitats – rivers, streams, lakes, marshes, and even burrows in damp soil. This *Aeshna* dragonfly larva is eating a stickleback underwater.

All dragonfly larvae catch prey using a structure called a "mask". In insects, one section of the mouthparts is called the labium, or lip. In dragonfly larvae this is enlarged to form the mask. While waiting to strike, the larva holds the mask folded back under its head. When a victim approaches close enough, the mask shoots out at incredible speed. On the end of the mask are two curved hooks, which dig into the prey. The larva then pulls the mask back in again.

Growing and changing

Dragonfly larvae change gradually as they grow. They **moult** ten to twenty times between hatching and becoming adults. Shortly before its final moult, a dragonfly larva stops feeding and climbs out of the water. The last larval skin splits, and an adult dragonfly emerges.

An adult dragonfly emerging from its last larval skin. Adults usually emerge at night or early in the morning, to avoid birds and other predators.

Giant fossils

Scientists have found fossils from about 300 million years ago of insects similar to modern dragonflies. One kind, called Meganeura, had a wingspan of 75 centimetres (30 inches), about the width of an open newspaper.

Not quite adults

Newly emerged dragonflies are not fully adult because they are not yet able to **mate**. For a short time (anything from a day to a month), they leave the water and fly inland to feed and mature. During this time they also develop their bright adult colours.

Darters, skimmers, and hawkers

Adult dragonflies are successful predators because they are superb fliers and they have excellent eyesight. True dragonflies can fly backwards, hover, and loop the loop, and many species are fast fliers. It is not unusual for the larger species to reach speeds of 30 kilometres (19 miles) per hour. Damselflies are not quite such strong fliers.

All dragonflies catch their prey on the wing, but they do not all hunt the same way. Most damselflies, and some dragonflies (for instance darters and skimmers) hunt from a perch. They sit on a lookout post and dart out on short flights when they spot prey. Other dragonflies (hawkers) patrol the air looking for prey, and rarely land on a perch.

Nearly all dragonflies will eat anything they catch. They often hunt among clouds of midges or other flies in the early evening.

Dragonflies have the largest compound eyes of any insect. In true dragonflies the eyes may meet in the middle, while in damselflies (as here) the eyes are wide apart.

Compound eyes

Dragonflies have very large eyes. As in most other insects, these are compound eyes. This means that each eye is made up of many separate "eyelets" – up to 30,000 of them in a dragonfly.

A dragonfly's compound eyes give excellent all-round vision and they are very good at spotting movement. Unlike human eyes, insect eyes can even see in **ultraviolet** light.

Mating and egg laying

When they are ready to mate, many dragonfly males look for an area of water to claim as their territory. They patrol their patch constantly, and chase off other males that try to invade their space. The males that have territories get more chances to mate with females.

After mating, females lay their eggs on or near water. Some dragonflies scatter their eggs on the water surface. Others have an egg-laying tube on the end of the abdomen, which they use to lay eggs inside plant stems. The females of one species of damselfly dive underwater for as long as an hour to lay their eggs.

This female southern hawker dragonfly is laying eggs. In some species of dragonfly the male helps by keeping watch for predators, or actually lifting the female away from the water after egg-laying.

Mantids

In a forest in Costa Rica, a dead leaf hangs from a thin branch. It sways slightly and looks as if it might fall. Just below, a beetle hurries along another branch. As the beetle approaches, the "leaf" shoots out two long, spiny arms. They grab the beetle and lift it towards the small triangular head that has now appeared. A South American boxing mantis has claimed another victim.

With their superb **camouflage**, mantids are probably the insect world's best sit-and-wait **predators**. There are about 2000 **species** of mantid worldwide. They are found in warmer parts of the world, especially in the **tropics**. Most mantids are medium to large insects – the biggest are around fifteen centimetres (six inches) long.

Praying for prey

Mantids are often called praying mantises, because they sit with their long front legs folded under the chin as if they are praying. But as one scientist said, all they are praying for is lunch!

A mantid's forelegs are its main weapons. They are long and covered in spikes, which makes it difficult for **prey** to escape. A mantid's jaws look small, but they are very strong and can quickly chop up a grasshopper or other large insect.

Mantids have a wide-ranging diet – they will eat whatever prey comes along. Most of their prey are insects, spiders, or other minibeasts, but some of the largest mantids catch frogs and small birds.

A mantid may remain motionless waiting for prey or it may sway gently, like a twig in the breeze. After a meal, a mantid will clean itself as carefully as a cat.

Looking sharp

Like dragonflies, mantids rely mainly on their eyesight to spot prey. The top of a mantid's triangular head is taken up by two large compound eyes. When a mantid sees prey approaching, it slowly turns its head to track the prey's movements. A mantid can turn its head more than half-way around. It can keep prey in sight without moving its body.

When the victim moves within range, the mantid shoots out its long front legs with tremendous speed. Mantids are so fast that they can often pluck a fly from the air if it comes within range.

Mantids sometimes hunt hanging from a perch rather than sitting on it.

Insect gladiators

Scientists have recently discovered a new kind of insect in southern Africa that does not fit in to any of the known insect groups. The new insects, known as gladiators, or heelwalkers, look like stick insects, but they are predators and catch prey with their front legs like mantids. They are called heelwalkers because they do not walk on the very ends of their legs like other insects, but on their "heels".

Masters of disguise

One reason why mantids are such successful predators is because they blend in so well with their background. In some cases this simply involves being a similar colour to their environment. Many mantids in tropical forests are green to blend in with the leaves. In some tropical areas, the leaves dry out and turn brown in the dry season. Where this happens, the mantids turn brown in the dry season, too.

Some mantids have far more elaborate disguises than just colouring. There are mantids that look like twigs, and others that look like dead leaves. In some desert areas there are short, rounded mantids that look like pebbles. And some tropical mantids look astonishingly like flowers. When they are young, these mantids can even change their "flower" colour to match the plant they are on.

Camouflage protects a mantid from predators, such as lizards and birds, as well as allowing it to surprise its prey.

Insect camouflage

Many insects rely on camouflage, to hide them from enemies. Some use protective colouring – for instance some moths match perfectly with tree bark or other backgrounds. Other insects, such as leaf and stick insects, actually look like leaves or sticks. Some bugs have large spikes on their backs that look like thorns. As well as providing camouflage, the spikes make the bugs difficult to eat.

Dangerous mates

Mantids spend most of their time alone, and treat anything that moves as possible prey. This makes it difficult for male mantids when they want to **mate** with a female. Male mantids are smaller than females, and risk being eaten when they get close enough to a female to mate.

In one mantid species, the European praying mantis, females do quite often eat males after mating. However, in most mantid species the males have ways of persuading the females not to attack. When he wants to mate with a female, the male moves towards her in a slow, wiggling dance. He has to avoid any sudden moves, or he will end up as her lunch!

Eggs and young

Female mantids lay groups of eggs in a protective case. They can produce several batches of eggs after just one mating. In a few species the female guards the egg case until the eggs hatch.

The young mantids that hatch from the eggs look like small, wingless versions of the adults. Within a short time these mini-mantids are hunting for themselves. Many young mantids are eaten by predators before they are fully grown. These predators include other mantids – even sometimes their own brothers and sisters!

Young mantids **moulting**. Mantids moult six or seven times between hatching and becoming adults.

13

Assassin bugs

It is early summer in a backyard in Brisbane, Australia. The air is filled with the scent of flowers and the buzzing of honeybees. A honeybee lands on a clump of flowers and begins to drink the nectar. While the bee is drinking, a reddish-brown insect creeps up and suddenly stabs the bee with its long, curved beak.

To most of us a bug is any kind of insect or creepy crawly, but to a scientist bugs are a specific **order** of insects, all of which have long, needle-like mouthparts. Many bugs are plant eaters, but assassin bugs are **predators**. Most assassin bugs live in **tropical** areas, but there are a few species in warm or **temperate** parts of the world.

Liquid food

Some assassin bugs are sit-and-wait predators, but others are more active and **stalk** their **prey**. Both kinds have front legs with spines or sticky pads, to grab and hold their prey. They also have a strong, curved beak, which they stab into their victims.

The assassin bug eats by injecting its prey with a mixture of saliva and poison. The poison **paralyses** the victim, while the saliva turns the victim's insides into a liquid. The assassin bug then sucks up this liquid, leaving the prey as just a dry husk.

Ways of hunting

Wheel bugs are large assassin bugs that live on shrubs and trees in North America. They prey on caterpillars and other insects. They get their name from a strange spiky "cogwheel" that sticks up from their back behind the head.

There are about 6500 species of assassin bugs ranging in size from about 7 to 40 millimetres (0.3 to 1.5 inches). They have a curved "beak" rather than straight mouthparts.

Like this wheel bug, many assassin bugs have hairs or spikes on their body, to stop them becoming food for another animal. When danger threatens, they also spray irritating saliva at their attacker.

Most assassin bugs hunt alone, but one kind found in Namibia, Africa, seems to work in groups. These bugs prey on millipedes ten times bigger than themselves. Groups of bugs attack the millipede together. Their combined poison quickly overpowers the millipede, then the assassins share the feast.

Young assassins

Female assassin bugs usually lay their eggs in cracks or under rocks. In tropical areas the eggs hatch in 20 days or so, but in cooler areas the eggs may take several months to hatch.

Blood-sucking assassins

Most assassin bugs are predators, but a few species are parasites that live on the blood of other animals. One group of blood-suckers are called cone-nose bugs. Most cone-noses are found in Central and South America, and a few species feed on human blood. Their bite is painful, and they can sometimes cause serious disease.

Like dragonflies and mantids, bugs grow by gradual metamorphosis. They take five or six moults to grow into adults.

Water bugs

A female damselfly has been underwater laying her eggs. As she struggles to the surface, four long-bodied insects come scooting across the surface towards her. The damselfly is bigger than them, but she is wet and tired from her long dive. The water striders all stab their needle-like beaks into her body. Within a few seconds their poison does its work, and the damselfly is still.

Assassin bugs are land **predators**, but there are other **families** of bugs that hunt in or on the water. As with assassin bugs, these water-based bugs feed by injecting their prey with a mixture of poison and saliva to paralyse prey and **dissolve** their insides.

Surface tension

Water striders are able to walk on water because the water surface acts as if it has a very thin "skin". This is known as surface tension. It is possible for small, light animals to walk on this skin, if they spread their weight over the surface. A water strider's long legs do this very well. For humans, however, walking on water would be much more difficult. To spread out our weight enough, we would need feet 2.5 kilometres (1.5 miles) long!

This water strider has caught a fly. Like other bugs, water striders develop by **gradual metamorphosis**.

Water striders

Pond skaters, or water striders, live on the surface of water rather than in it. There are about 500 kinds, ranging in size from 1.5 to 36 millimetres (from 0.05 to 1.5 inches). They have long, thin bodies, long legs to spread their weight over the water, and they are covered in tiny water-repellent hairs that help them stay afloat. They move by sculling themselves over the surface with their middle legs, using their back legs to steer.

Water striders live mainly on still water, and feed on insects that fall on the water and get trapped.

Hunting by feel

Water striders have sense organs on their legs that pick up **vibrations** in the water. When they sense the vibrations of an insect struggling at the surface, they rush to the spot. A water strider uses its short front legs to hold on to its **prey** while it injects its long **mouthparts** into its victim's body. Like assassin bugs, water striders suck their victims dry.

Water striders lay their eggs on floating plants or other floating objects. If the water level falls while the eggs are developing, the hatching **larvae** are not left high and dry. In cold areas water striders survive winter by hiding away in hollow plant stems or other winter retreats. A kind of "antifreeze" in their blood protects their bodies against ice formation.

Water crickets are closely related to water striders. They are generally smaller than water striders and are short-bodied. This one has caught a wasp.

Backswimmers

Backswimmers, sometimes called water boatmen, are a group of bugs that live just below the water surface rather than on it. As their name suggests, backswimmers swim on their backs. The ends of their long back legs are covered in stiff hairs, making a pair of "oar blades". The backswimmer "rows" through the water with oar-like back legs, and uses its strong front legs for grabbing prey. The backswimmer has large eyes right on the top of its head. Because it swims on its back, it can see forwards, backwards, and down into the water as it swims along looking for prey.

Like other bug predators, backswimmers inject a mixture of saliva and paralysing poison into their victims. This means that despite their small size, no bigger than 17 millimetres (just over 0.5 inches) long, backswimmers catch and kill prey as large as young fish. Their poisonous bite is also painful for humans!

Backswimmers are lighter than water, and float to the surface if they stay still. They have to actively swim down to stay under the water.

Sea skaters

Insects are successful on land and in fresh water, but very few insects can survive at sea. However, sea skaters, which belong to the water strider family, live on the surface of the sea rather than on fresh water. Sea skaters have been seen feeding on **plankton**, dead jellyfish, and fish eggs. They lay their eggs on floating objects, such as shells, pieces of wood, and lumps of tar.

Although they live in water, backswimmers have to breathe air. They do this in two ways. They can trap a certain amount of air around long hairs on their body. They also have a long breathing tube on the end of their **abdomen**, which they can poke above the surface to get a new air supply.

Despite living underwater, adult backswimmers have wings and can fly. This allows them to move on if an area of water dries up or if prey become scarce.

Giant water bugs

Giant water bugs truly are insect giants – the largest **species** can be 110 millimetres (almost 4.5 inches) long. This makes them the largest water-living insects. Like other backswimmers they swim with their back legs, and use their front legs to grab and hold prey while they inject their victims with venom and saliva.

Giant water bugs hunt by stealth, hiding among water plants and **ambushing** their prey. They eat other water insects, tadpoles, and small fish. Because of their size, a giant water bug's bite is extremely painful to humans.

Giant water bugs can fly and, when they are ready to **mate**, they fly from pond to pond looking for a partner. At these times they are often attracted to electric lights, like giant moths.

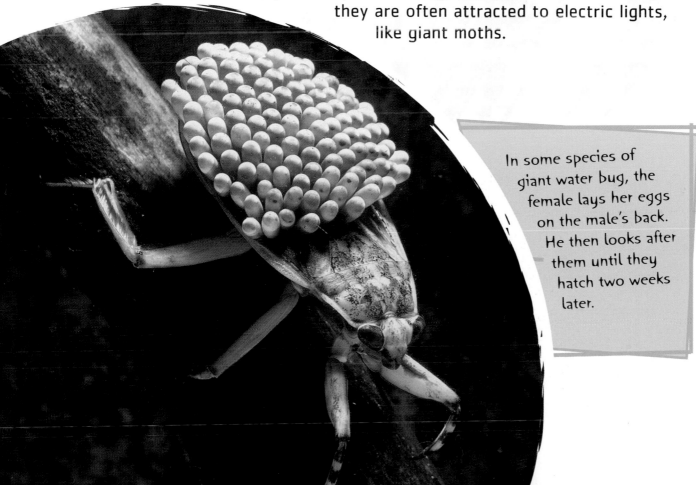

In some species of giant water bug, the female lays her eggs on the male's back. He then looks after them until they hatch two weeks later.

Lacewings, ant lions, and snakeflies

A small insect with huge, saw-tooth jaws wanders through the sandy soil of a French forest. Its tracks look like a child's doodle in the sand. But then there is a change – the insect begins to move slowly inwards in a spiral, scooping up sand and throwing it outwards as it goes. After about ten minutes, the insect is in the centre of the spiral, at the bottom of a steep-sided pit. An ant lion has dug its deadly trap.

Snakeflies, lacewings, ant lions, and their relatives belong to a group of insects called the Neuroptera ("nerve-wings"). They get this name from the net-like pattern of veins in their wings. The **larvae** of neuropterans look very different from the adults. They change from larvae to adults by **complete metamorphosis**.

Lacewings

There are about 5000 different species of lacewings and their relatives. Green lacewings eat pollen and nectar, but many other types of adult lacewings, and all lacewing larvae, are fierce **predators**. They hunt aphids, mites, and other plant-eating insects.

Adult lacewings hunt at night, creeping up silently in the dark then pouncing on their victims. But lacewing larvae hunt by day. Some larvae camouflage themselves by sticking pieces of soil to their bodies. Others cover themselves with the skins of their dead **prey**, sticking them to spikes on their bodies.

These adult lacewings have ears in their wings! They use them to listen for bats, which are their main enemies.

Singing lacewings

Male green lacewings "sing" to attract a mate by vibrating their abdomens. This produces a low-pitched sound that vibrates the leaves they are standing on. The vibrations travel to other parts of the plant, and any female that feels them vibrates back. The male keeps up his vibrating song as he goes looking for the female.

Other insects also use sound to attract mates. The loudest "singers" are cicadas, a kind of plant-eating bug. The chirruping song of a cicada can be heard over 1.5 kilometres (nearly a mile) away!

Ant lions

Ant lions are close relatives of lacewings. Adult ant lions look similar to small dragonflies, but they are much weaker fliers and hunt at night.

Ant lions get their name from their larvae, which are ferocious predators. Some live on tree trunks or burrow into soil. Most live in sandy soil, and make traps to catch their prey. To make its trap, an ant lion larva digs a steep-sided pit in the sand. It then buries itself in the sand at the bottom of the pit, leaving only its head and saw-tooth jaws sticking out.

An ant lion larva's body is covered in forward-pointing bristles. This means that even large prey cannot pull the ant lion out of the ground once it has grabbed them.

Ant lion adults are similar to dragonflies, but their antennae are longer and have knobs on the end.

Springing the trap

When an ant or other insect comes along, it loses its footing on the soft edge of the trap and falls in. The ant lion larva then grabs the trapped victim using **pincer** jaws. If the prey tries to climb out of the pit, the ant lion larva picks up sand grains and throws them at the escaping prey. The victim then loses its footing and falls back into the ant lion's jaws.

The larva's curved, pincer-like jaws are hollow. It feeds in a similar way to assassin bugs, injecting saliva to turn the prey's insides into liquid, then sucking this liquid up.

Some mantispids specialize in hunting spiders – even deadly ones, such as black widows! The one in the picture has caught itself a fly.

Owlflies and mantispids

Two other lacewing relatives that are predators are owlflies and mantispids. Owlfly larvae look similar to ant lions, although they do not dig traps. The adults are much stronger fliers than adult ant lions, and they catch prey on the wing. Owlflies can sometimes be mistaken for dragonflies, but they have long antennae whereas dragonfly antennae are short.

Insects in amber

Amber is sticky sap from trees that grew millions of years ago. It has formed into hard, transparent yellow material. Many pieces of amber contain fossil insects, including snakeflies. The insects were trapped in the sticky resin millions of years ago and have been beautifully preserved in the amber.

Mantispids are similar to small mantids. A mantispid has a long "neck", a mobile head, and strong, grasping front legs. Like mantids, they hunt by ambushing their prey. Some mantispids are disguised as social wasps (wasps that live in groups), and hunt the wasps whose appearance they mimic.

Snakeflies

Snakeflies are found everywhere except Australia. The flies get this name because their heads are on a long, snake-like "neck". Females look even more snake-like because their body ends in a long, curved egg-laying tube.

Snakeflies are forest insects. Most of them live high in the forest **canopy**. The main prey of adult snakeflies are aphids (greenfly) and the caterpillars of butterflies and moths. A snakefly runs down its prey, then shoots out its long "neck", like a striking snake grabbing its victim.

Female snakeflies use their egg-laying tube to lay eggs under the bark of trees. The larvae live under the tree bark, hunting prey such as young bark beetles. The larvae take about two years to reach full growth. They then spin silk cocoons and become **pupae**. After a few days, an adult snakefly emerges from each pupa.

Snakeflies are a fairly small group of insects. There are about 200 known species.

Ladybirds

It is spring in the Sierra Nevada Mountains of California. Everywhere you look, ladybirds are appearing – from tree stumps, from piles of old leaves, or from cracks in rocks. The ladybirds hibernated in autumn last year. Now they are taking to the air in great swarms and heading for farmlands in California's Central Valley. Here they can find plenty of aphids and other tasty **prey**.

Ladybirds are probably the best known kind of beetle – but there are thousands of others! There are over 300,000 beetle species, which is more than a third of all the animal species in the world. The thing that all beetles have in common is that their front wings are not used for flying. Instead they have become a pair of tough wing cases, which protect the delicate back wings. Most beetles are plant eaters or **scavengers**, but apart from one small group of plant eaters, all ladybirds are **predators**.

A ladybird's bright colours are a warning to predators that ladybirds do not make good food. If attacked, they produce a very unpleasant yellow liquid.

Ladybirds

There are over 5000 different kinds of ladybirds. The most familiar ones are red, yellow, or orange with black or white spots. All ladybirds have a very round shape, with short legs and antennae. They are popular with farmers because they eat aphids (greenfly), fruit flies, mites, and other tiny plant-sucking insects that damage food crops.

Ladybird adults and larvae both have sharp **mandibles** for grabbing and chewing up their prey. They find prey mainly through scent. Aphids move slowly and are often found in large groups, so they are fairly easy to catch.

Ladybird larvae are grey when they first hatch, but as they grow they develop warning spots, like the adults.

Like all beetles, ladybirds go through **complete metamorphosis** as they grow. Female ladybirds lay their eggs on plants where aphids or other suitable prey are found. The **larvae** that hatch look different from the adults, but they eat the same kinds of prey. The larvae have tremendous appetites, and can get through hundreds of aphids in the ten to thirty days it takes them to reach full size.

Larvae **moult** three or four times, then after a final moult turn into **pupae**. Between three and twelve days later, an adult ladybird climbs out of the pupa. Adult ladybirds live several weeks or months, depending on where they live and the time of year.

Natural pest killers

Ladybirds are often used by farmers to save their crops from plant pests. For example, farmers growing oranges and lemons in Florida, USA, release thousands of ladybirds, known as "mealy bug destroyers", in their orchards each year. These ladybirds kill and eat pests called mealy bugs that can damage or destroy the orange and lemon trees.

Tiger beetles and ground beetles

A tiger beetle larva sits with just its head poking out of the soil, watching out for passing **prey**. The rest of its soft body is hidden below ground. Another beetle walking past comes too close to the larva's hiding place. The larva reaches out and grabs the beetle in its jaws. The beetle struggles and tries to escape, but hooks on the back of the larva's **abdomen** keep it safely anchored in its tunnel home.

Tiger beetles and ground beetles are closely related, fast-moving predatory beetles. Ground beetles are usually night hunters, but tiger beetles hunt by day.

Tiger beetles

Tiger beetles have large eyes which give them excellent eyesight for spotting prey. Tiger beetles are extremely fast on their feet. Some can move at speeds of over 60 centimetres (24 inches) per second. This may not seem fast, but if the beetle was as big as a human it would be able to run 50 metres (165 feet) in less than a second!

Tiger beetles are most likely to be seen on sunny days, hunting on open ground. They are fast enough to run down most prey, including other beetles, caterpillars, ants, flies, and grasshoppers.

One way of telling tiger beetles from ground beetles is that the large eyes of tiger beetles make a tiger beetle's head wider than its thorax.

Tiger beetles are also excellent fliers. They may sometimes make short flights when chasing a victim. Once they catch up with their prey, their large **mandibles** make short work of the victim.

Young tigers

Tiger beetles lay their eggs in the soil. When an egg hatches, the larva digs up to the surface, using its head and **thorax** like a shovel to carry the soil. The larvae stay in the burrow they have dug for themselves, ambushing and eating passing prey. The larvae enlarge and lengthen their burrow as they grow.

After three **moults**, the larvae **pupate** in their burrow. When the adult tiger beetle emerges, it may continue to use the burrow as a place to sleep at night.

A bombardier produces its spray by mixing two chemicals in a special chamber in its abdomen. When the chemicals mix they heat up and shoot out of one end of the chamber.

Beetle explosions

Some ground beetles and tiger beetles produce a horrible-smelling liquid if they are attacked, and others can produce chemicals that blister the skin. But one group of ground beetles, the bombardier beetles, have a truly amazing defence mechanism. If a bombardier beetle is under threat, it produces an explosive, burning spray. The spray comes out so fast it makes a popping noise. The bombardier can aim the spray at its attacker using a nozzle on the end of its abdomen, and fire off up to twenty explosive spray charges in quick succession.

Ground beetles

Ground beetles are one of the biggest beetle families. There are at least 40,000 known kinds. The shiny black beetles that scurry away if you turn over a stone or old leaves are likely to be ground beetles.

In **temperate** countries ground beetles are usually shiny black or brown, but in **tropical** areas they are often brightly coloured. In many ground beetles the wing cases are joined together down the middle, and the beetle cannot fly.

These ground beetles have managed to catch a snail to eat.

Ground beetles are fast movers that actively seek out their prey. Some species hunt any kind of soft-bodied prey, such as slugs, caterpillars, worms, and grubs. Often they hunt at night, using their antennae to follow the trail of chemicals that slugs, for instance, leave behind them as they move. Like tiger beetles, their large mandibles make short work of their prey.

Specialist eaters

Not all ground beetles eat a range of prey – some are more choosy. Searcher beetles, for instance, eat mainly caterpillars, often going high into trees to find them. In tropical forests, searchers and other ground beetles do not live on the ground at all! They hunt insect prey high in the forest canopy.

Another group of specialists are snail-hunting ground beetles. Some snail-hunters have mouthparts like hooks, which they use to winkle the snail out of its shell. Others have a long, narrow heads that poke right inside the shell. They then pour saliva on to the snail's soft body to **digest** it, and suck up the resulting snail broth.

Farmers' friends

Like ladybirds, ground beetles help farmers and gardeners by eating pest insects that ruin their plants. Some kinds of ground beetle have been used by farmers to protect their crops from specific pests. The fiery searcher beetle, for instance, was introduced into the USA from Europe because it eats the caterpillars of gypsy moths. Gypsy moths were accidentally introduced to the United States from Europe, and their caterpillars cause serious damage to trees.

Fierce larvae

Ground beetle larvae are also fierce **predators**. They look quite worm-like, but they have pincer jaws for attacking insects. Many kinds of ground beetles lay their eggs in the soil. The larvae that hatch out live for up to a year below ground, hunting worms, insects, and other soil creatures. They then **pupate** in the soil. When the adult beetle emerges from the pupa it digs its way to the surface to begin hunting and looking for a **mate**.

Fiery searchers are very large ground beetles, up to 4 centimetres (1.5 inches) long.

Giant diving Beetles

At the surface of a shallow stream, a giant diving beetle comes up for air. It lifts the back of its abdomen out of the water for a few moments, then dives again. A space under the beetle's wing covers acts like a diver's aqualung, trapping air that the beetle can breathe while it is underwater looking for tadpoles or other juicy **prey**.

Some beetle species are **predators** in water rather than on land. There are over 4000 **species** of diving beetles around the world. Some can be as small as 1.5 millimetres (less than 0.05 inches), but giant diving beetles are over 40 millimetres (about 1.5 inches) long.

Hairy oars

Giant diving beetles are fierce predators. They eat water insects but also snails, tadpoles, frogs, and fish bigger than the beetles themselves. Small prey are swallowed whole, but the beetles tear larger prey to pieces with their strong jaws. Adult giant diving beetles are excellent swimmers. Their bodies are highly streamlined to help them slip easily through the water, while stiff hairs on their back legs act like oars to push them along. They search for prey among water plants.

A diving beetle's front legs are used to grab and hold prey, while its middle legs are used to hold on to underwater plants when resting.

Although diving beetles live in water, they do not have gills and must breathe air. Hairs along the sides of the **abdomen** help them to trap air under their wing cases, allowing them to carry their own air supply.

Even though they spend most of their lives underwater, adult diving beetles can still fly. This allows them to leave a dried-up pond, or to leave an area if prey are scarce.

In places with cold winters, diving beetles survive by burying themselves in mud at the bottom of a pool and **hibernating**. They can slow their bodies down enough to live through the winter buried in the mud.

Water tigers

Female diving beetles lay their eggs one at a time in the stems of water plants. The eggs hatch out into **larvae** called water tigers. A water tiger has a long, S-shaped body with two curved tubes on the end of the abdomen. The curved tubes are breathing tubes. The larva hangs from the water surface with just the tips of its breathing tubes in the air, and waits for prey such as mosquitoes or midge larvae, water fleas, or tadpoles.

When water tigers are fully grown, they crawl on shore and find a damp place near the shore where they can **pupate**. When the adult beetle emerges from the pupa, it returns to the water.

When a water tiger catches prey, it uses its curved, hollow jaws to inject saliva into the prey and dissolve its insides. The water tiger then sucks up the soupy mixture.

Predatory flies

A silver weaver spider has begun building a new web. As it spins the web's "spokes", a robber fly appears. The fly buzzes around the web, watching the spider. Then it dives in, lands on the spider's back and stabs its mouthparts into the spider's body. The spider hardly has time to struggle before the poison in the fly's mouthparts paralyses it.

There are about 120,000 known **species** of true flies. Robber flies are one of several fly **families** that are **predators**.

Robber flies

Robber flies are designed for catching **prey** on the wing. They have excellent eyesight, and long, bristly legs good for grabbing prey in mid-air. They use their short, knife-like mouthparts to stab the **thorax**, or body, of their prey.

Robber flies catch all kinds of prey, including large, dangerous insects such as wasps, bees, dragonflies, and spiders. Most robber flies hunt from a perch. They fly out when they see prey approaching, grab it with their long legs, and stab their mouthparts into the victim's body. The poison that the fly injects stops the victim from struggling, and the saliva **dissolves** its insides.

Female robber flies lay their eggs in the soil. The **larvae** that hatch out are white and look like worms. They hunt and eat worms and the larvae of other insects they find in the soil.

Robber flies are the biggest of all the true flies. They can be up to eight centimetres (three inches) long. They live in all parts of the world, but prefer dry, open areas and hot weather.

Long-legged flies are a group of smaller predators that hunt over water. They are usually bright metallic blue or green and, as their name suggests, they have long legs.

Dance flies

Dance flies look like smaller, slimmer versions of robber flies. Whereas robber flies have short, stabbing mouthparts, dance flies have much longer, slim "daggers". There are about 3000 dance fly species worldwide. They live near rivers, lakes, ponds, or the seashore.

Dance flies hunt on the wing in a similar way to robber flies. Dance fly larvae are also predators. Some live in soil or in **leaf litter**, while other larvae live in water.

Dance flies get their name from the way that males attract females for **mating**. Groups of males gather together over water and fly in a twisting, spiralling "dance" to attract the attention of females.

Flying aces

Many kinds of insects are called flies, but true flies are a specific group of insects that all have only a single pair of flying wings. The back wings have been modified into two club-shaped structures, called halteres, that help balance. Having only one pair of wings does not make true flies poor flyers – in fact, flies are flying aces. They can turn on a pinhead, hover, fly backwards, and even land upside down!

A male dance fly. Male dance flies use a "gift" of a fly or other insect to try and attract a female. In some species the male wraps his gift in silky thread spun from **glands** on his front legs.

Wasps

A mantid stands motionless on a bush, poised to grab **prey**. A small black and red wasp flies by, and the mantid turns its head to watch. The wasp begins to fly rapidly back and forth, just out of reach of the mantid's deadly front legs. After a time, the mantid seems to lose track of the wasp's movements. Then the wasp darts in and stings three times – once to paralyse the forelegs, and twice more for the rest of the body.

Wasps belong to the order Hymenoptera – the wasps, ants, and bees. About 36,000 hymenopteran species are hunting wasps. Some species live and hunt alone, but other wasps are social and live in large groups.

Some hunting wasps attack large, fierce predators, such as mantids or this wolf spider. They can fly short distances carrying even these large prey.

Powerful weapons

Wasps are among the insect world's most deadly **predators**. They have strong legs, biting jaws, and they are excellent fliers with sharp senses for finding prey. A wasp's main weapon is its sting. Its narrow, flexible "waist" allows a wasp to aim its sting with great accuracy, even while holding struggling prey.

Nectar eaters

Adult wasps are not actually meat-eaters – they live on nectar from flowers. However, female wasps hunt insects or spiders to feed their **larvae**, which are meat-eaters. The females make a nest or burrow, fill it with "provisions", then lay one or more eggs. When the eggs hatch, they have a food supply ready to eat.

Different ways of hunting

The poison in a wasp's sting can kill its prey, but many wasps only **paralyse** their victims. This way the prey that the wasps provide for their larvae do not rot and go bad before the larvae hatch out and eat them.

Many wasps hunt a wide range of prey, but some kinds specialize. Some digger wasps catch only grasshoppers, while others specialize in mantids. Pompilus wasps are spider specialists. There are also weevil hunters, fly hunters, and wasps that hunt **cicadas**.

Parasitic wasps

Some wasps do not build nests and catch food for their offspring – they are parasites that lay their eggs directly on to or into another animal (the host). When the eggs hatch, they feed on the tissues of their host. At first this has little effect, but as the larvae grow they injure and eventually kill their host. The host may be an insect egg, a caterpillar or other insect larva, an adult insect, or a spider, depending on the kind of parasitic wasp.

Different kinds of wasps build different nests. Some use existing holes or cracks, and some dig tunnels in the ground. Other wasps make nests from daubed mud, like this potter wasp.

Bee wolves

Bee pirates, or bee wolves, are a group of wasps that specialize in hunting bees. They grapple their prey tight with their legs and sting it in the neck. Although the bee may sting back, it can only reach the protected back of the wasp's **abdomen**, so its stings have no effect.

Bee wolves kill their prey outright rather than paralysing them. This is because they return to the nest and feed their larvae as they grow, rather than leaving food and abandoning them.

Once a bee wolf has killed its prey, it squeezes the victim to push out all the honey the bee has stored in its **crop**. The adult licks up the honey, then feeds the corpse of the bee to one of its young.

There are about 1100 different species of bee wolves and their relatives. While the one in the picture is preying on a honey bee, some species prey on ants and others hunt beetles.

Social wasps

The best known kinds of wasps, such as "yellowjackets" or common wasps, are social wasps that live together in a large group or colony. A social wasp colony builds a nest containing hundreds or thousands of cells, each one containing an egg or a wasp larva.

Common wasps make their nests from wood, which they chew and mix with saliva to make a kind of tough paper.

A wasp colony is begun by one female wasp – a queen. She builds a small nest and lays a number of eggs that grow into workers – female wasps that cannot lay eggs. The worker wasps take over the jobs of enlarging the nest, catching food, and feeding new larvae, leaving the queen to lay eggs. The workers feed the larvae on chewed-up prey.

In **temperate** climates, the wasp colony produces workers through the spring and summer. Then in autumn it begins to raise male wasps and new queens. As winter approaches the new queens mate, then find sheltered places where they can survive the winter. The rest of the wasp colony dies, leaving the young queens to start again next year.

Killer bees were bred in Brazil by scientists trying to develop an improved type of honey bee. Some bees escaped, and they have gradually spread north to the USA.

"Killer" bees

Bees are closely related to social wasps, but they feed their larvae on honey rather than on insects. The honey bees that we raise to produce honey have been bred for gentleness, but in parts of the southern USA a new kind of honey bee has begun to appear. These killer bees are a cross between honey bees and wild African bees. Like other bees they will sting only if they feel threatened, but killer bees are more easily upset than ordinary bees. Although it is very rare for anyone to die from a killer bee attack, an angry swarm can sting a person hundreds of times in just a few seconds.

Hunting ants

The quiet of a forest in Central America is broken by noise – the twittering of ant birds, the buzzing of many flies and the rustling hiss of countless insects fleeing for their lives. On the ground, a mass of red-black ants, several metres wide, moves slowly forwards. As the ants travel, they kill everything in their path. A column of army ants is on the move.

Ants are the most successful **predators** of the insect world. They eat more **prey** than any other group of insects. There are over 11,000 different ant **species**, all of which live in large groups, known as colonies.

Wasp and bee relatives

Ants are close relatives of wasps and bees. Some eat leaves or seeds, and some are **omnivores**, but many ant species are predators.

Like wasps, many ants have two sets of weapons to attack their prey – biting jaws and a poisonous sting. Some kinds of ant do not have a sting, but instead have a different weapon – a spray of **acid**.

The life of an ant colony

A typical ant colony begins in late summer, when huge numbers of male and female winged ants take flight at about the same time. The female ants are young queens, and they **mate** in flight with several males. Each queen then lands and rubs off her wings – they will be of no further use as she will spend the rest of her life underground. She then digs a hole that is the beginning of a new ant nest.

Wood ants live in large nest mounds in cool parts of the northern hemisphere. Wood ant queens do not start a new colony alone – they join an existing colony.

Ant senses

Some ants have reasonable eyesight, and all ants can make and hear high-pitched sounds. But ants live mainly in a world of smell and taste. Ants use their antennae or mouthparts to pick up scents in the air, or "tastes" on the ground or on other ants. Members of a particular colony recognize each other by smell. Hunting trails are marked out with long-lasting scents, while an ant in trouble will release a fast-acting alarm scent, which soon brings other ants running.

The young queen lays her first batch of eggs, which hatch into worker ants (wingless female ants that do not mate). Some of the workers go out and look for food, while others take over care of the eggs, **larvae** and **pupae**.

The queen continues to lay eggs, and the colony slowly grows. Once the colony reaches a certain size, the workers raise a group of winged males and young queens, ready for the next mating flight.

Ants work together on the tasks of finding food, feeding the young, building a nest, and defending from enemies. Here one worker gives food it has caught to another ant.

Ant hunters

In the simplest kinds of ant colonies, worker ants go out alone to hunt for prey. Each worker attacks any prey she finds, biting and stinging it. She then carries the food back to the nest.

However, in most ant colonies workers do not hunt by themselves. When they look for food, they usually follow trails laid down on previous hunting trips. As they travel, workers mark the trails with scent. Other workers can then follow their route.

One of the large "soldier" ants that guard an army ant colony. Its jaws are so huge that it cannot use them to feed. Soldiers are fed by worker ants in the colony.

If a worker finds prey, she may simply kill it and carry it back to the nest. However if the prey is large, or if there are several prey animals, the worker heads back to the nest, laying a new kind of scent trail that tells other workers, "Food this way!" Whenever the worker meets another ant from her nest, she waves her head and touches antennae to tell the other ant about the food. Soon a crowd of ants are heading towards the food source.

Bulldog ants from Australia are examples of ants that are solo hunters. These large, fierce ants will fearlessly attack humans who come too close to their nests.

Ant juggernauts

A few ant species hunt not just in groups, but as a huge mass. Army ants in South America and driver ants in Africa both hunt in this way. Army and driver ants do not live in nests. Instead, they protect their queen, eggs, larvae, and pupae with their own bodies, by forming a huge ball around the queen in some sheltered spot. This is called a bivouac.

Each day, a column of ants heads out from the bivouac, attacking and killing any prey animals in their way. Some ants return with the food, while other ants push the front of the column forwards. As it grows, the column begins to branch and spread. Insects, spiders, worms, snails, even frogs and chicks, are killed and carried back to the bivouac. The ants overwhelm many prey by sheer numbers, but there are also some giant ants guarding the front and sides of the column – up to 500 times bigger than the smallest ants in the colony!

At the end of the day the column retreats for the night, ready to head out in a new direction the next day.

Ant farmers

In some hunting ant species the workers kill prey to feed the ant larvae, but they themselves live on sugary foods, such as nectar. Insects, such as aphids (greenfly), produce a sweet, sugary substance known as honeydew. Wood ants keep "herds" of aphids and feed on their honeydew. In return for the honeydew, the ants protect the aphids from predators.

A wood ant "herding" a group of aphids.

Specialist hunters

Most ants are general predators, and will kill any prey that they can catch. However some species specialize in catching particular prey.

One group of ants, known as dacetines, specialize in catching small, wingless insects called springtails. Springtails can jump away quickly when in danger – to catch them, dacetines have fast-acting "mousetrap" jaws. These long, thin jaws can be opened right out like a pair of very wide pincers. When a dacetine ant gets close to a springtail she jerks her head forward, and sensitive trigger hairs on the jaws make them snap shut extremely quickly.

Ants are tremendously strong. They can run carrying prey that weigh more than themselves, and drag much larger prey.

Another ant with strange jaws lives in **tropical** forests in the Americas. The jaws have huge spikes on them, like the prongs of a pitchfork. The ant uses these pitchfork jaws to catch a millipede that is covered in long bristles – a kind of insect porcupine. The ant spears the millipede with her jaws, then uses hairs on the pads of her forefeet to strip the bristles off before eating her prey.

Thieves and slave-takers

Most ant species work hard to build their nests and find food, but a few have found ways of avoiding work. Colonies of thief ants, for instance, live close to colonies of other ants, and steal food from these neighbouring ants.

Some ant species go one step further and steal other ants! Large red or black Amazon ants, for instance, raid the nests of wood ants and steal wood ant pupae. The captured wood ants do all the work in the Amazon ant colony.

The end of a colony

Most worker ants live short lives – some die only two weeks after emerging from the pupa. However, the ant colony itself lasts much longer. Many colonies last as long as the founding queen is alive, which can be fifteen years or more, depending on the species. Soon after she dies the colony dies, too. However, during the queen's lifetime the colony will have sent out many young queens to start new colonies.

In a few ant species, colonies do not die with the old queen. For instance when a wood ant queen mates, she does not start her own nest but goes back to her home nest. The large wood ant nests, which can house over a million ants, have several queens rather than just one. When a colony gets too big, a whole group of workers, plus one or two fertile queens, move out and start a new nest mound nearby.

Most ant colonies have nests underground or in trees. However, some "ant plants" grow special structures for ants to use as nests. In return, the ants defend the plants from enemies.

classification chart

Scientists classify living things (sort them into groups) by comparing their characteristics (their similarities and differences). A **species** is a group of animals or plants that are all similar and can breed together to produce young. Similar species are put together in a larger group called a **genus** (plural genera). Similar genera are grouped into families, and so on through bigger and bigger groupings – **classes**, **orders**, phyla, and kingdoms. Plants and animals are the two major kingdoms.

Insects belong to the class Insecta. There are over a million known insect species in 28 orders. The main insect orders are listed below.

Genus	Number of families	Number of species
Mayflies (Ephemeroptera)	19	2000
Dragonflies (Odonata)	27	6000
Cockroaches (Blattodea)	6	3500
Termites (Isoptera)	7	2300
Mantids (Mantodea)	8	1800 to 2000
Earwigs (Dermaptera)	10	1900
Stoneflies (Neoptera)	15	2000
Crickets & grasshoppers (Orthoptera)	39	22,000
Leaf & stick insects (Phasmatodea)	6	2500
Parasitic lice (Pterygota)	26	3150
Bugs (Hemiptera)	136	82,000
Lacewings (Neuroptera)	20	5000
Beetles (Coleoptera)	166	300,000
Fleas (Siphonaptera)	16	1800
Flies (Diptera)	155	120,000
Caddisflies (Trichoptera)	43	7000
Butterflies & moths (Lepidoptera)	127	180,000 to 200,000
Wasps, bees & ants (Hymenoptera)	106	120,000

Insect body parts and life cycles

Parts of an insect

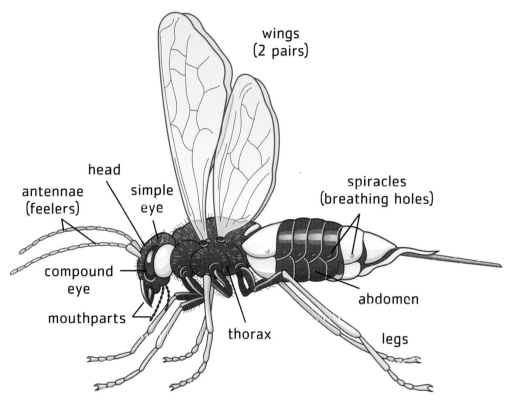

wings
(2 pairs)

head

antennae
(feelers)

simple
eye

spiracles
(breathing holes)

compound
eye

mouthparts

thorax

abdomen

legs

Insect life cycles

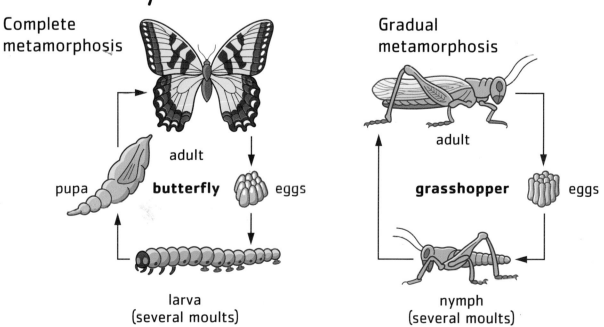

Complete
metamorphosis

adult

pupa

butterfly

eggs

larva
(several moults)

Gradual
metamorphosis

adult

grasshopper

eggs

nymph
(several moults)

Glossary

abdomen back part of the body of a spider or insect

ambush wait in hiding to attack prey

camouflage colouring and markings on an insect or other animal that help it blend in with its background

canopy leafy tops of forest trees

cicada kind of large, stout-bodied bug

class grouping of living things made up of one or more closely related orders

cocoon protective silky case spun by some insect larvae

complete metamorphosis a kind of change found in insects such as beetles, butterflies, bees and wasps, in which the young insect (larva) is very different from the adult. The larva turns first into a pupa, then into an adult.

crop part of the insect gut before the stomach where food can be stored

cuticle material that makes up the hard outer shell of an insect

digest to break down food into useful chemicals that the body can use for energy and to grow

dissolve to mix with a liquid until it becomes part of the liquid

family grouping of living things made up of one or more closely related genera

genus (plural genera) a grouping of living things made up of one or more closely related species

gradual metamorphosis a kind of metamorphosis found in insects such as grasshoppers and bugs, in which the young insect changes gradually into an adult as it grows and moults

hibernate to go into a deep sleep through the winter

larva (plural larvae) young stage of an insect

leaf litter layer of dead and rotting leaves on the floor of a wood or forest

mandibles bones of the lower jaws

mating when a male and a female animal come together to produce young

metamorphosis way that an insect or animal changes as it grows.

midges small biting flies often found near water

moult to shed the outer skin to reveal a new skin beneath

mouthparts mandibles (jaws), palps ('lips') and other parts of an insect's mouth

nymph young stage of an insect that looks similar to its parents

omnivore animal that eats both plants and other animals

order grouping of living things that consists of one or more closely related families

paralyse a paralysed animal is unable to move

pincer claw that can pinch

plankton tiny animals and plants found in the ocean that drift with the currents

predator animal that hunts and eats other animals

prey animal that is hunted by a predator

pupa (plural pupae) stage in some insects' lives when a larva forms a protective case in which it turns into an adult

pupate to form a pupa

scavenger animal that eats dead and rotting meat, and other waste material

species group of animals that are similar and can breed together to produce healthy offspring.

stalk to creep up on prey

temperate in a temperate place the climate is mild (neither very hot nor very cold)

thorax middle part of an insect's body

tropics/tropical lands around the Equator where the climate is very warm all year

ultraviolet type of high-energy light that humans cannot see

vibrations shaking or ripples

Further information

Books

See Through Science: Insects, David Burnie (Heinemann Library, 1995)
An in-depth look at the hidden world around us.

Collins Complete British Insects, Michael Chinery (Collins, 2004)
If you want to look for insects in Britain, this is the book to help you.

Field Guide to Insects Coloring Book, (Peterson Field Guide Colouring Books)
Robert Michael Pyle, Kristin Kest (Houghton Mifflin, 1993)
Alternatively, you could colour your own insects!

Classifying Living Things: Insects, Andrew Solway (Heinemann Library, 2003)
Explores the key features and characteristics of insects and how each one
is different from the rest.

Websites and organizations

www.earthlife.net/insects/six.html
Interesting information about all the insect groups, and some links to other
websites (although some of these no longer work).

www.enchantedlearning.com/subjects/insects/printouts.shtml
Clear and simple information and drawings of insects.

www.museums.org.za/bio/insects/mantophasmatodea/
Information about the newest insect order.

www.ento.vt.edu/~sharov/3d/3dinsect.html
Insect animations and information.

www.blackmask.com/books29c/mhtgw.htm#1_0_3
J. Henri Fabre was a great 19th century naturalist. His second book on
wasps, available online, is full of fascinating stories based on direct
observation. Definitely worth the effort of getting used to the old-
fashioned language.

Index

Titles in the *Wild Predators!* series include:

Hardback 0431189927

Hardback 0431189943

Hardback 0431190070

Hardback 0431190038

Hardback 0431190054

Hardback 0431189951

Hardback 0431190046

Hardback 0431190062

Hardback 0431189935

Hardback 0431189919

Find out about the other titles in this series on our website www.heinemann.co.uk/library